Date _____   Source of Anxie⁺ ~~~~

Time _____   Physical Sensat

Place _____

Negative Beliefs

About Yourself	About Situation

What facts do you know are true?

About Yourself	About Situation

Color where you feel
sensations of anxiety

Is there a more balanced way to think about this situation

What has helped before?

What is helping now?

Coping Mechanisms

Breathe
Remind yourself that anxiety is just a feeling
Describe your surroundings in detail
Go outdoors
Sip a warm or iced drink slowly
Ground yourself

This Week's Goals

What I would like to learn

How I will have fun

Kind things I can do

Places I would like to go

How I will feed my brain

How I will care for my body

Stop stressing about...

Ideas

Conversations

Shopping list

-
-
-
-
-
-
-
-
-
-

Things to do

Explore and learn about...

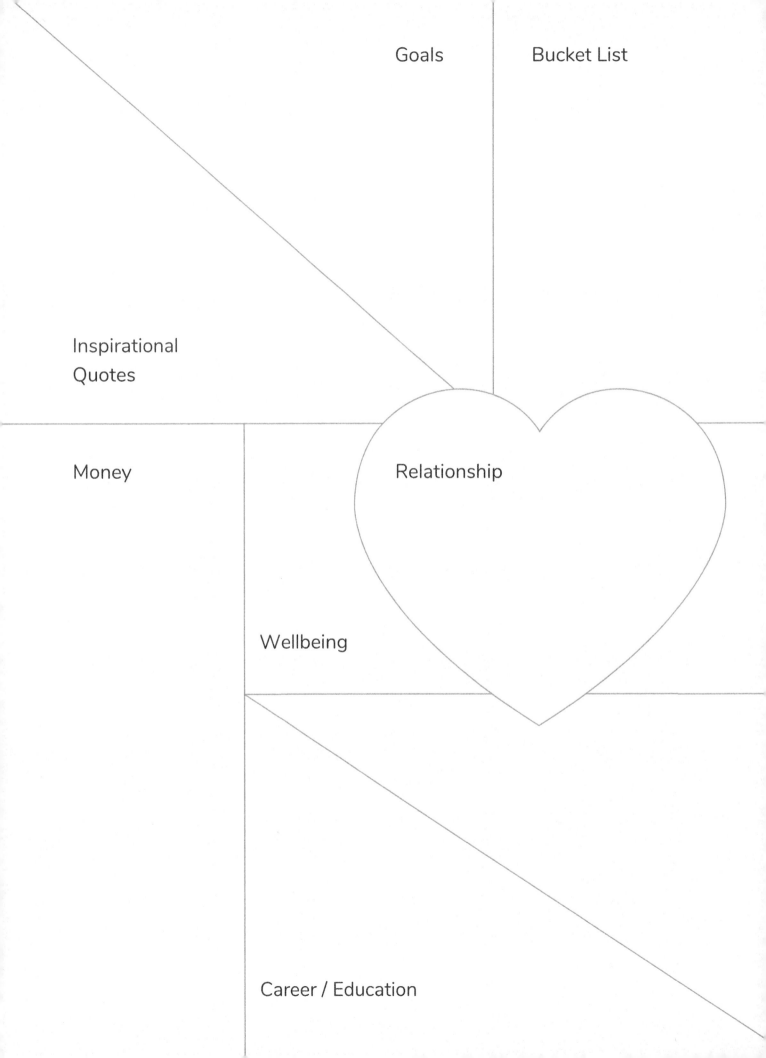

Goals

Bucket List

Inspirational
Quotes

Money

Relationship

Wellbeing

Career / Education

Relationship Communications

Problem I would like to solve

My desired outcome

What do I feel
about this issue?

What do I think my partner feels
about this issue?

What do I feel I need to do to
solve this problem?

What do I feel my partner needs
to do to solve this problem?

What would I like my partner to do today

What I would like to do today

What obstacles are
in our way?

What strategies can we use to
overcome the obstacles?

What I would like to
tell my partner

Happy Memory Clouds

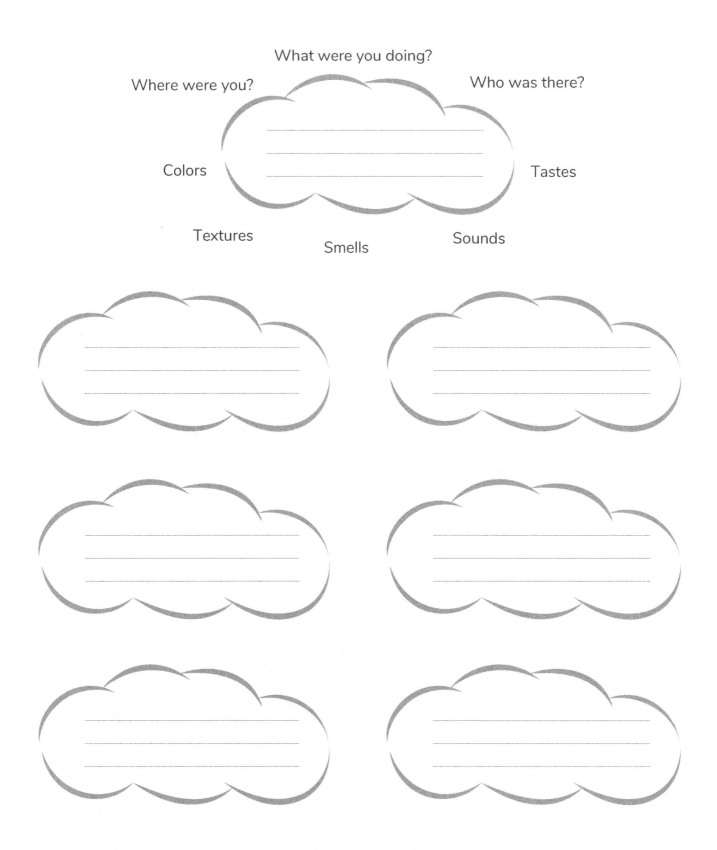

What were you doing?

Where were you?

Who was there?

Colors

Tastes

Textures

Smells

Sounds

Fill out these clouds as you think of happy memories.
Use them when your emotions become overwhelming.

Finger Labyrinth

Use your finger to slowly trace a path to the center of the labyrinth

Breathe calmly and slowly as you focus.
When you reach the center, draw a long deep breath or two.

Then trace your path back to the outside
Repeat until you feel more focused and calm.

Focus Words

Breathe - Peace - Relax - Tranquility - Serenity - Calm - Space - Beauty
Love - Wonder - Kindness - Light - Happiness - Joy - Warmth

Observations

Letting Go
Self Criticism

Critical Thought

"I should…"
"I can't believe…"
"I wish…"
"I'm so stupid"

What triggered this thought?

"I was late to the meeting"
"I forgot to call my mom"
"My friend stood me up"

Physical and Emotional Sensations

How does this thought
make you feel?

Compassionate Thought

What you might say if a
friend expressed this
thought

A year from now

How will you feel about
this event next year?
Will it matter?

Concrete Plan

What action can you
take to prepare for
this in future.

Big picture plan

Imagine a future free
from this thought.
What will you do?

Date _____   Source of Anxiety _____

Time _____   Physical Sensations _____

Place _____

Negative Beliefs

About Yourself	About Situation

What facts do you know are true?

About Yourself	About Situation

Color where you feel
sensations of anxiety

Is there a more balanced way to think about this situation

What has helped before?

What is helping now?

Coping Mechanisms

Breathe
Remind yourself that anxiety is just a feeling
Describe your surroundings in detail
Go outdoors
Sip a warm or iced drink slowly
Ground yourself

Self Care Routine

Vision _____

Time	Step

Routine Notes

Food _____

_____

Spiritual _____

_____

Exercise _____

_____

Mantra _____

Daily Tracker

1	2	3	4	5	6	7	8	9	10
11	12	13	14	15	16	17	18	19	20
21	22	23	24	25	26	27	28	29	30
31	Start Date :				End Date :				

Date _____   Source of Anxiety _____

Time _____   Physical Sensations _____

Place _____

Negative Beliefs

About Yourself	About Situation

What facts do you know are true?

About Yourself	About Situation

Color where you feel
sensations of anxiety

Is there a more balanced way to think about this situation

What has helped before?

What is helping now?

Coping Mechanisms

Breathe
Remind yourself that anxiety is just a feeling
Describe your surroundings in detail
Go outdoors
Sip a warm or iced drink slowly
Ground yourself

This Week's Goals

What I would like to learn

How I will have fun

Kind things I can do

Places I would like to go

How I will feed my brain

How I will care for my body

Stop stressing about...

Ideas

Conversations

Shopping list
-
-
-
-
-
-
-
-
-
-

Things to do

Explore and learn about...

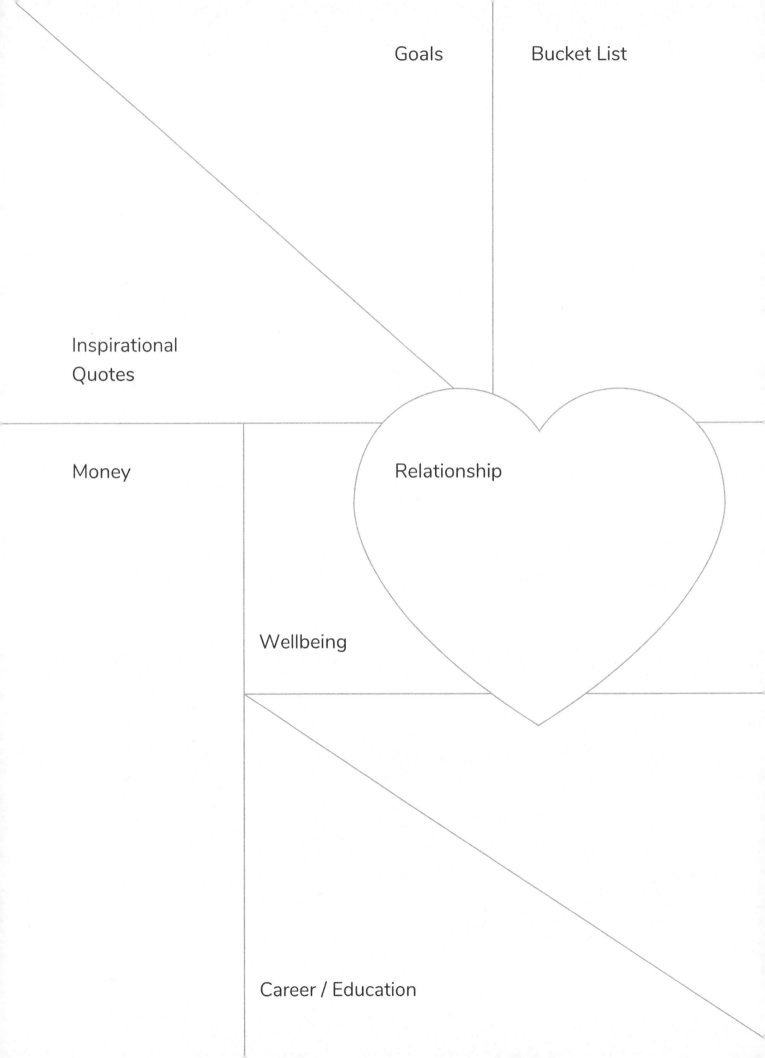

Goals

Bucket List

Inspirational
Quotes

Money

Relationship

Wellbeing

Career / Education

Relationship Communications

Problem I would like to solve

My desired outcome

What do I feel
about this issue?

What do I think my partner feels
about this issue?

What do I feel I need to do to
solve this problem?

What do I feel my partner needs
to do to solve this problem?

What would I like my partner to do today

What I would like to do today

What obstacles are
in our way?

What strategies can we use to
overcome the obstacles?

What I would like to
tell my partner

Happy Memory Clouds

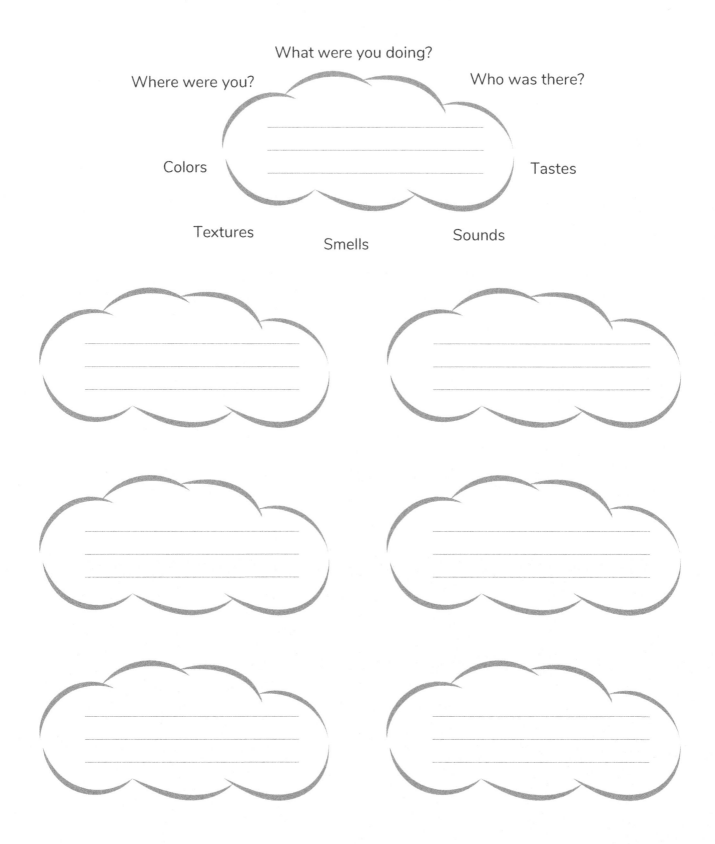

Where were you?
What were you doing?
Who was there?

Colors
Tastes

Textures
Smells
Sounds

Fill out these clouds as you think of happy memories.
Use them when your emotions become overwhelming.

Finger Labyrinth

Use your finger to slowly trace a path to the center of the labyrinth

Breathe calmly and slowly as you focus.
When you reach the center, draw a long deep breath or two.

Then trace your path back to the outside
Repeat until you feel more focused and calm.

Focus Words

Breathe - Peace - Relax - Tranquility - Serenity - Calm - Space - Beauty
Love - Wonder - Kindness - Light - Happiness - Joy - Warmth

Observations

Letting Go
Self Criticism

Critical Thought

"I should…"
"I can't believe…"
"I wish…"
"I'm so stupid"

What triggered this thought?

"I was late to the meeting"
"I forgot to call my mom"
"My friend stood me up"

Physical and Emotional Sensations

How does this thought
make you feel?

Compassionate Thought

What you might say if a
friend expressed this
thought

A year from now

How will you feel about
this event next year?
Will it matter?

Concrete Plan

What action can you
take to prepare for
this in future.

Big picture plan

Imagine a future free
from this thought.
What will you do?

Date _____

Time _____

Place _____

Source of Anxiety _____

Physical Sensations _____

Negative Beliefs

About Yourself	About Situation

What facts do you know are true?

About Yourself	About Situation

Color where you feel
sensations of anxiety

Is there a more balanced way to think about this situation

What has helped before?

What is helping now?

Coping Mechanisms

Breathe
Remind yourself that anxiety is just a feeling
Describe your surroundings in detail
Go outdoors
Sip a warm or iced drink slowly
Ground yourself

Self Care Routine

Vision _____

Time	Step

Routine Notes

Food _____

_____

Spiritual _____

_____

Exercise _____

_____

Mantra _____

Daily Tracker

1	2	3	4	5	6	7	8	9	10
11	12	13	14	15	16	17	18	19	20
21	22	23	24	25	26	27	28	29	30
31	Start Date :				End Date :				

Date _____   Source of Anxiety _____

Time _____   Physical Sensations _____

Place _____

Negative Beliefs

About Yourself	About Situation

What facts do you know are true?

About Yourself	About Situation

Color where you feel
sensations of anxiety

Is there a more balanced way to think about this situation

What has helped before?

What is helping now?

Coping Mechanisms

Breathe
Remind yourself that anxiety is just a feeling
Describe your surroundings in detail
Go outdoors
Sip a warm or iced drink slowly
Ground yourself

This Week's Goals

What I would like to learn

How I will have fun

Kind things I can do

Places I would like to go

How I will feed my brain

How I will care for my body

Stop stressing about...

Ideas

Conversations

Shopping list

-
-
-
-
-
-
-
-
-

Things to do

Explore and learn about...

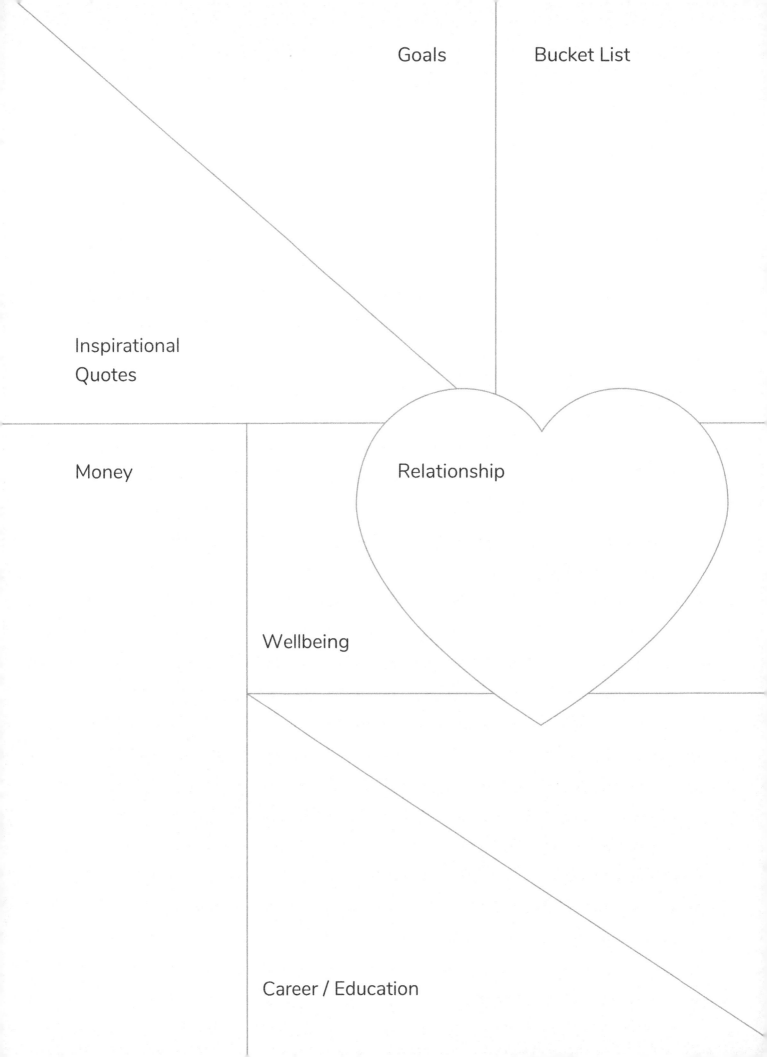

Goals

Bucket List

Inspirational
Quotes

Money

Relationship

Wellbeing

Career / Education

Relationship Communications

Problem I would like to solve

My desired outcome

What do I feel
about this issue?

What do I think my partner feels
about this issue?

What do I feel I need to do to
solve this problem?

What do I feel my partner needs
to do to solve this problem?

What would I like my partner to do today

What I would like to do today

What obstacles are
in our way?

What strategies can we use to
overcome the obstacles?

What I would like to
tell my partner

Happy Memory Clouds

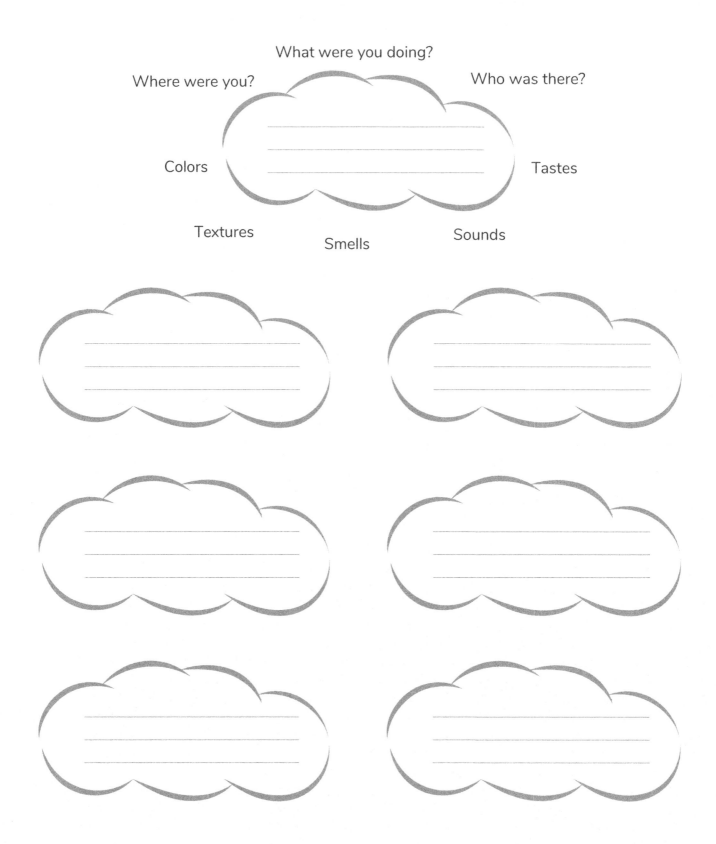

What were you doing?

Where were you?

Who was there?

Colors

Tastes

Textures

Smells

Sounds

Fill out these clouds as you think of happy memories.
Use them when your emotions become overwhelming.

Finger Labyrinth

Use your finger to slowly trace a path to the center of the labyrinth

Breathe calmly and slowly as you focus.
When you reach the center, draw a long deep breath or two.

Then trace your path back to the outside
Repeat until you feel more focused and calm.

Focus Words

Breathe - Peace - Relax - Tranquility - Serenity - Calm - Space - Beauty
Love - Wonder - Kindness - Light - Happiness - Joy - Warmth

Observations

Letting Go
Self Criticism

Critical Thought

"I should..."
"I can't believe..."
"I wish..."
"I'm so stupid"

What triggered this thought?

"I was late to the meeting"
"I forgot to call my mom"
"My friend stood me up"

Physical and Emotional Sensations

How does this thought
make you feel?

Compassionate Thought

What you might say if a
friend expressed this
thought

A year from now

How will you feel about
this event next year?
Will it matter?

Concrete Plan

What action can you
take to prepare for
this in future.

Big picture plan

Imagine a future free
from this thought.
What will you do?

Date _____   Source of Anxiety _____

Time _____   Physical Sensations _____

Place _____

Negative Beliefs

About Yourself	About Situation

What facts do you know are true?

About Yourself	About Situation

Color where you feel
sensations of anxiety

Is there a more balanced way to think about this situation

What has helped before?

What is helping now?

Coping Mechanisms

Breathe
Remind yourself that anxiety is just a feeling
Describe your surroundings in detail
Go outdoors
Sip a warm or iced drink slowly
Ground yourself

Self Care Routine

Vision _____

Time	Step

Routine Notes

Food _____

_____

Spiritual _____

_____

Exercise _____

_____

Mantra _____

Daily Tracker

1	2	3	4	5	6	7	8	9	10
11	12	13	14	15	16	17	18	19	20
21	22	23	24	25	26	27	28	29	30
31	Start Date :				End Date :				

Date _____   Source of Anxiety _____

Time _____   Physical Sensations _____

Place _____

Negative Beliefs

About Yourself	About Situation

What facts do you know are true?

About Yourself	About Situation

Color where you feel
sensations of anxiety

Is there a more balanced way to think about this situation

What has helped before?

What is helping now?

Coping Mechanisms

Breathe
Remind yourself that anxiety is just a feeling
Describe your surroundings in detail
Go outdoors
Sip a warm or iced drink slowly
Ground yourself

This Week's Goals

What I would like to learn

How I will have fun

Kind things I can do

Places I would like to go

How I will feed my brain

How I will care for my body

Stop stressing about...

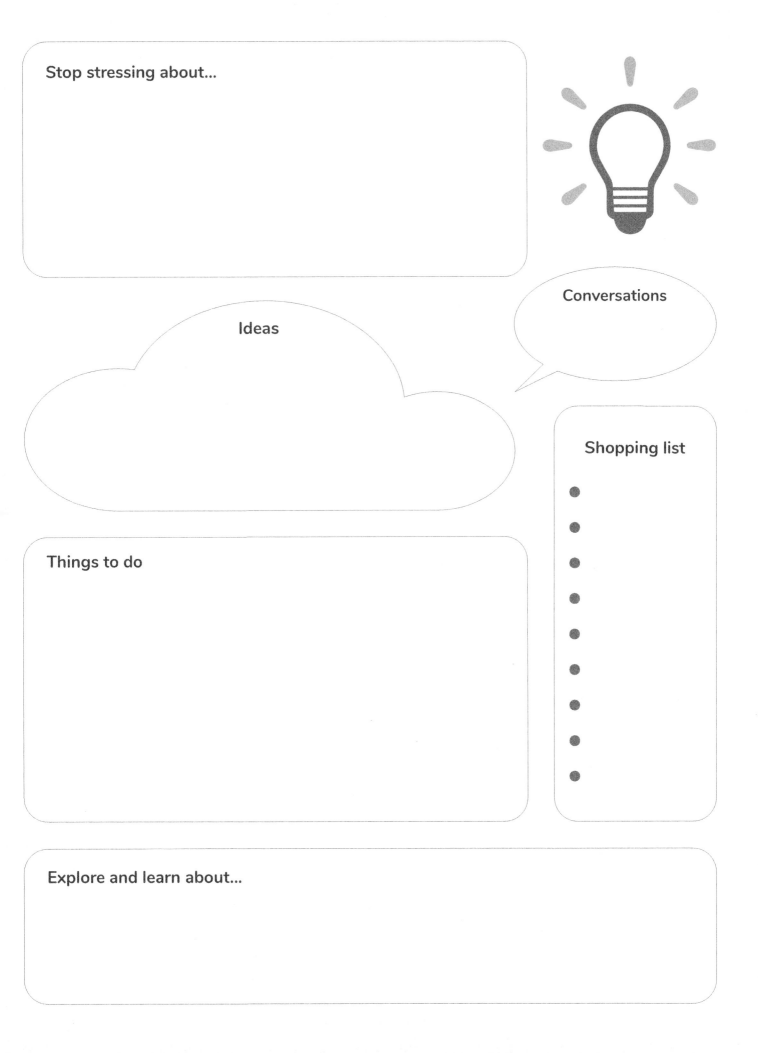

Ideas

Conversations

Shopping list

-
-
-
-
-
-
-
-
-
-

Things to do

Explore and learn about...

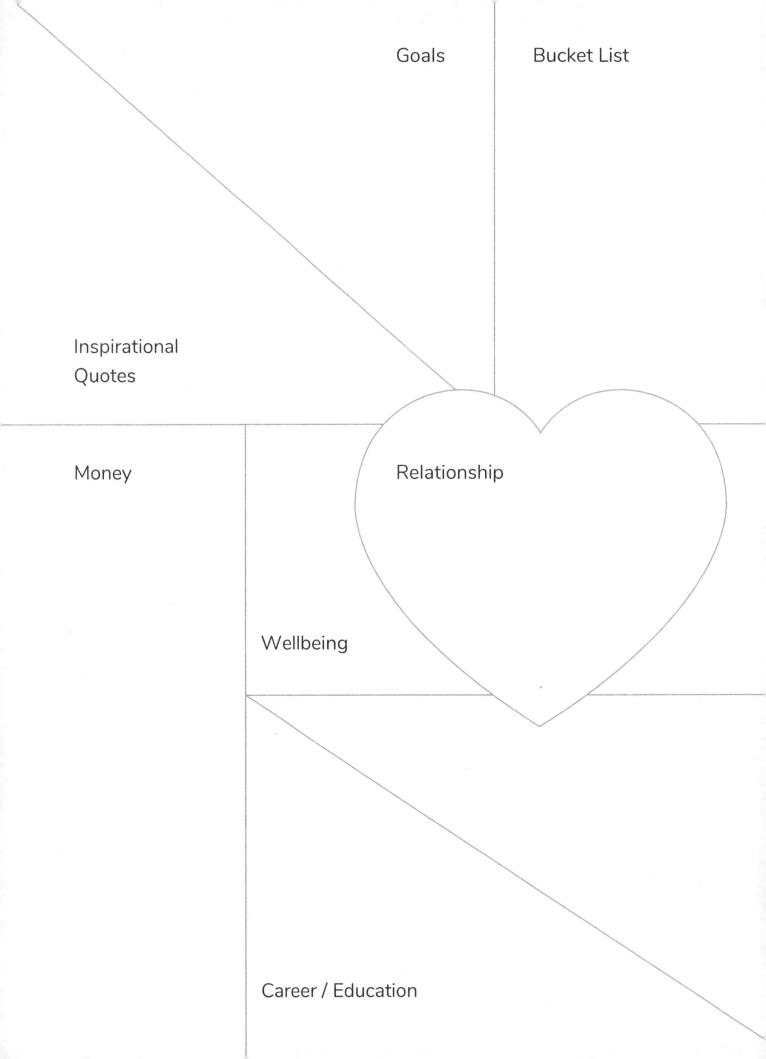

Goals

Bucket List

Inspirational
Quotes

Money

Relationship

Wellbeing

Career / Education

Relationship Communications

Problem I would like to solve

My desired outcome

What do I feel about this issue?

What do I think my partner feels about this issue?

What do I feel I need to do to solve this problem?

What do I feel my partner needs to do to solve this problem?

What would I like my partner to do today

What I would like to do today

What obstacles are in our way?

What strategies can we use to overcome the obstacles?

What I would like to tell my partner

Happy Memory Clouds

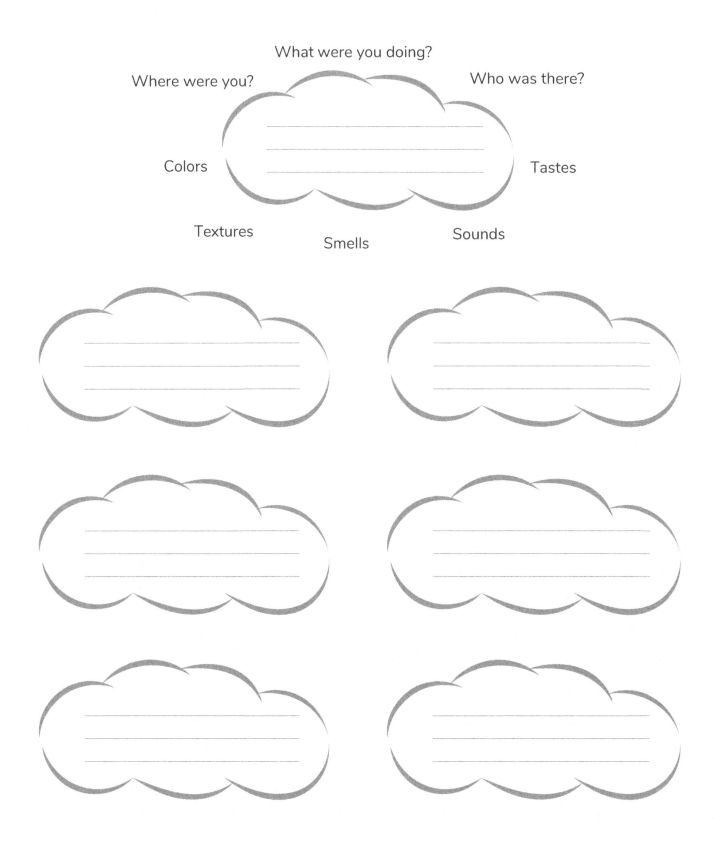

Where were you?   What were you doing?   Who was there?

Colors   Tastes

Textures   Smells   Sounds

Fill out these clouds as you think of happy memories.
Use them when your emotions become overwhelming.

Finger Labyrinth

Use your finger to slowly trace a path to the center of the labyrinth

Breathe calmly and slowly as you focus.
When you reach the center, draw a long deep breath or two.

Then trace your path back to the outside
Repeat until you feel more focused and calm.

Focus Words

Breathe - Peace - Relax - Tranquility - Serenity - Calm - Space - Beauty
Love - Wonder - Kindness - Light - Happiness - Joy - Warmth

Observations

Letting Go
Self Criticism

Critical Thought

"I should…"
"I can't believe…"
"I wish…"
"I'm so stupid"

What triggered this thought?

"I was late to the meeting"
"I forgot to call my mom"
"My friend stood me up"

Physical and Emotional Sensations

How does this thought
make you feel?

Compassionate Thought

What you might say if a
friend expressed this
thought

A year from now

How will you feel about
this event next year?
Will it matter?

Concrete Plan

What action can you
take to prepare for
this in future.

Big picture plan

Imagine a future free
from this thought.
What will you do?

Date _____   Source of Anxiety _____

Time _____   Physical Sensations _____

Place _____

Negative Beliefs

About Yourself	About Situation

What facts do you know are true?

About Yourself	About Situation

Color where you feel
sensations of anxiety

Is there a more balanced way to think about this situation

What has helped before?   What is helping now?

Coping Mechanisms

Breathe
Remind yourself that anxiety is just a feeling
Describe your surroundings in detail
Go outdoors
Sip a warm or iced drink slowly
Ground yourself

Self Care Routine

Vision _____

Time	Step

Routine Notes

Food _____

_____

Spiritual _____

_____

Exercise _____

_____

Mantra _____

Daily Tracker

1	2	3	4	5	6	7	8	9	10
11	12	13	14	15	16	17	18	19	20
21	22	23	24	25	26	27	28	29	30
31	Start Date :				End Date :				

Date _____   Source of Anxiety _____

Time _____   Physical Sensations _____

Place _____

Negative Beliefs

About Yourself	About Situation

What facts do you know are true?

About Yourself	About Situation

Color where you feel
sensations of anxiety

Is there a more balanced way to think about this situation

What has helped before?

What is helping now?

Coping Mechanisms

Breathe
Remind yourself that anxiety is just a feeling
Describe your surroundings in detail
Go outdoors
Sip a warm or iced drink slowly
Ground yourself

This Week's Goals

What I would like to learn

How I will have fun

Kind things I can do

Places I would like to go

How I will feed my brain

How I will care for my body

Stop stressing about...

Ideas

Conversations

Shopping list

-
-
-
-
-
-
-
-
-
-

Things to do

Explore and learn about...

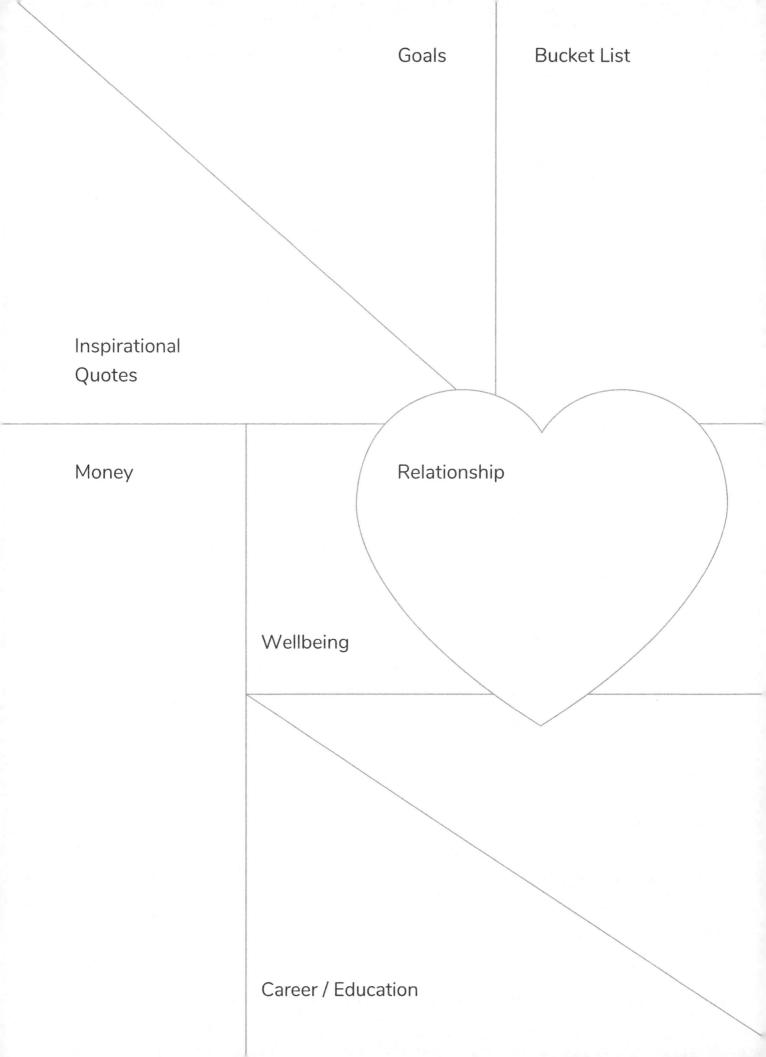

Goals

Bucket List

Inspirational
Quotes

Money

Relationship

Wellbeing

Career / Education

Relationship Communications

Problem I would like to solve

My desired outcome

What do I feel about this issue?

What do I think my partner feels about this issue?

What do I feel I need to do to solve this problem?

What do I feel my partner needs to do to solve this problem?

What would I like my partner to do today

What I would like to do today

What obstacles are in our way?

What strategies can we use to overcome the obstacles?

What I would like to tell my partner

Happy Memory Clouds

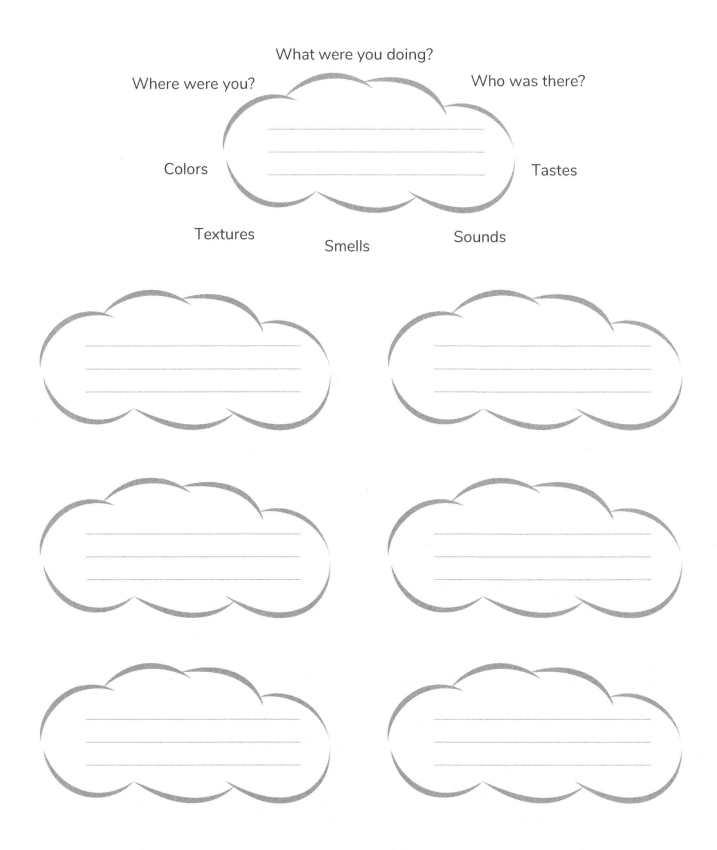

Fill out these clouds as you think of happy memories.
Use them when your emotions become overwhelming.

Finger Labyrinth

Use your finger to slowly trace a path to the center of the labyrinth

Breathe calmly and slowly as you focus.
When you reach the center, draw a long deep breath or two.

Then trace your path back to the outside
Repeat until you feel more focused and calm.

Focus Words

Breathe - Peace - Relax - Tranquility - Serenity - Calm - Space - Beauty
Love - Wonder - Kindness - Light - Happiness - Joy - Warmth

Observations

Letting Go
Self Criticism

Critical Thought

"I should…"
"I can't believe…"
"I wish…"
"I'm so stupid"

What triggered this thought?

"I was late to the meeting"
"I forgot to call my mom"
"My friend stood me up"

Physical and Emotional Sensations

How does this thought
make you feel?

Compassionate Thought

What you might say if a
friend expressed this
thought

A year from now

How will you feel about
this event next year?
Will it matter?

Concrete Plan

What action can you
take to prepare for
this in future.

Big picture plan

Imagine a future free
from this thought.
What will you do?

Date _____   Source of Anxiety _____

Time _____   Physical Sensations _____

Place _____

Negative Beliefs

About Yourself	About Situation

What facts do you know are true?

About Yourself	About Situation

Color where you feel
sensations of anxiety

Is there a more balanced way to think about this situation

What has helped before?   What is helping now?

Coping Mechanisms

Breathe
Remind yourself that anxiety is just a feeling
Describe your surroundings in detail
Go outdoors
Sip a warm or iced drink slowly
Ground yourself

Self Care Routine

Morning / Evening / Other

Vision _____

Time	Step

Routine Notes

Food _____

_____

Spiritual _____

_____

Exercise _____

_____

Mantra _____

Daily Tracker

1	2	3	4	5	6	7	8	9	10
11	12	13	14	15	16	17	18	19	20
21	22	23	24	25	26	27	28	29	30
31	Start Date :				End Date :				

Date _____

Time _____

Place _____

Source of Anxiety _____

Physical Sensations _____

Negative Beliefs

About Yourself	About Situation

What facts do you know are true?

About Yourself	About Situation

Color where you feel
sensations of anxiety

Is there a more balanced way to think about this situation

What has helped before?

What is helping now?

Coping Mechanisms

Breathe
Remind yourself that anxiety is just a feeling
Describe your surroundings in detail
Go outdoors
Sip a warm or iced drink slowly
Ground yourself

This Week's Goals

What I would like to learn

How I will have fun

Kind things I can do

Places I would like to go

How I will feed my brain

How I will care for my body

Stop stressing about...

Ideas

Conversations

Shopping list

-
-
-
-
-
-
-
-
-
-

Things to do

Explore and learn about...

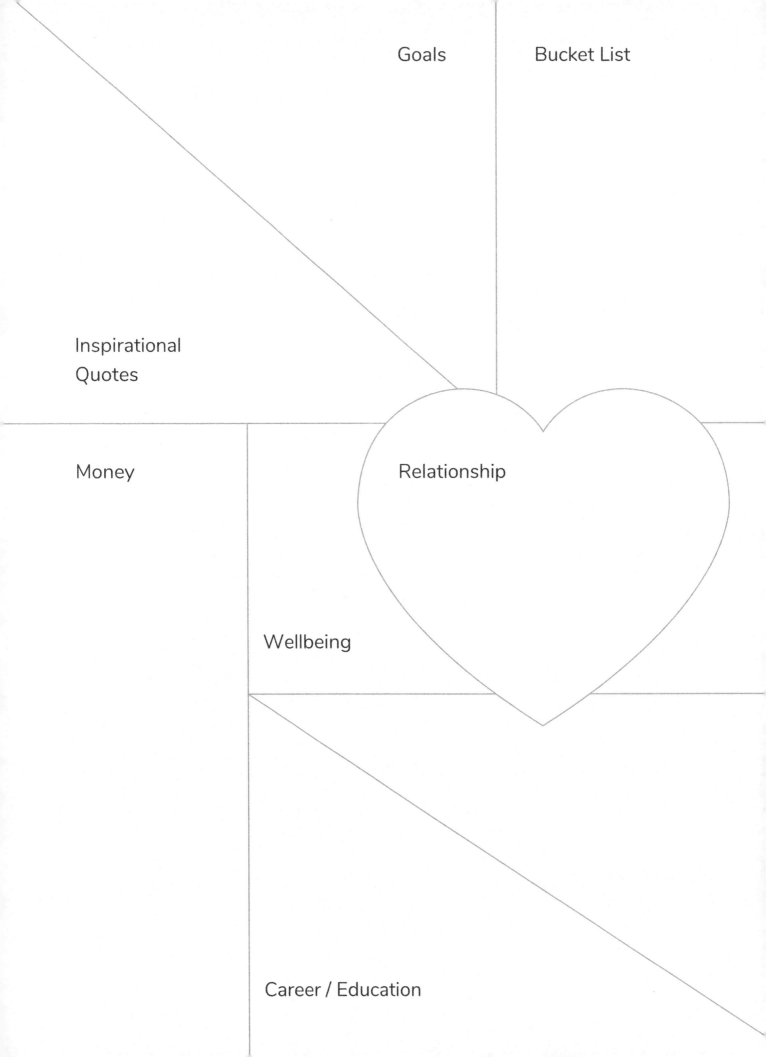

Goals

Bucket List

Inspirational
Quotes

Money

Relationship

Wellbeing

Career / Education

Relationship Communications

Problem I would like to solve

My desired outcome

What do I feel
about this issue?

What do I think my partner feels
about this issue?

What do I feel I need to do to
solve this problem?

What do I feel my partner needs
to do to solve this problem?

What would I like my partner to do today

What I would like to do today

What obstacles are
in our way?

What strategies can we use to
overcome the obstacles?

What I would like to
tell my partner

Happy Memory Clouds

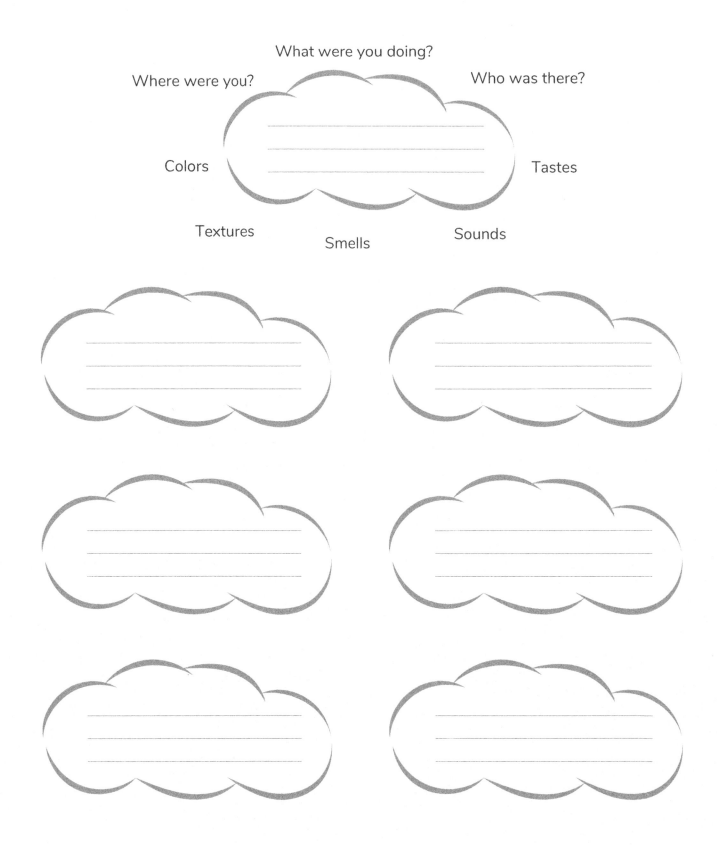

What were you doing?

Where were you?

Who was there?

Colors

Tastes

Textures

Smells

Sounds

Fill out these clouds as you think of happy memories.
Use them when your emotions become overwhelming.

Finger Labyrinth

Use your finger to slowly trace a path to the center of the labyrinth

Breathe calmly and slowly as you focus.
When you reach the center, draw a long deep breath or two.

Then trace your path back to the outside
Repeat until you feel more focused and calm.

Focus Words

Breathe - Peace - Relax - Tranquility - Serenity - Calm - Space - Beauty
Love - Wonder - Kindness - Light - Happiness - Joy - Warmth

Observations

Letting Go
Self Criticism

Critical Thought

"I should…"
"I can't believe…"
"I wish…"
"I'm so stupid"

What triggered this thought?

"I was late to the meeting"
"I forgot to call my mom"
"My friend stood me up"

Physical and Emotional Sensations

How does this thought
make you feel?

Compassionate Thought

What you might say if a
friend expressed this
thought

A year from now

How will you feel about
this event next year?
Will it matter?

Concrete Plan

What action can you
take to prepare for
this in future.

Big picture plan

Imagine a future free
from this thought.
What will you do?

Date _____   Source of Anxiety _____

Time _____   Physical Sensations _____

Place _____

Negative Beliefs

About Yourself	About Situation

What facts do you know are true?

About Yourself	About Situation

Color where you feel
sensations of anxiety

Is there a more balanced way to think about this situation

What has helped before?

What is helping now?

Coping Mechanisms

Breathe
Remind yourself that anxiety is just a feeling
Describe your surroundings in detail
Go outdoors
Sip a warm or iced drink slowly
Ground yourself

Self Care Routine

Vision _____

Time	Step

Routine Notes

Food

_____

_____

Spiritual

_____

_____

Exercise

_____

_____

Mantra

_____

Daily Tracker

1	2	3	4	5	6	7	8	9	10
11	12	13	14	15	16	17	18	19	20
21	22	23	24	25	26	27	28	29	30

31	Start Date :	End Date :

Date _____   Source of Anxiety _____

Time _____   Physical Sensations _____

Place _____

Negative Beliefs

About Yourself	About Situation

What facts do you know are true?

About Yourself	About Situation

Color where you feel
sensations of anxiety

Is there a more balanced way to think about this situation

What has helped before?

What is helping now?

Coping Mechanisms

Breathe
Remind yourself that anxiety is just a feeling
Describe your surroundings in detail
Go outdoors
Sip a warm or iced drink slowly
Ground yourself

This Week's Goals

What I would like to learn

Kind things I can do

How I will have fun

Places I would like to go

How I will feed my brain

How I will care for my body

Stop stressing about...

Ideas

Conversations

Shopping list

-
-
-
-
-
-
-
-
-

Things to do

Explore and learn about...

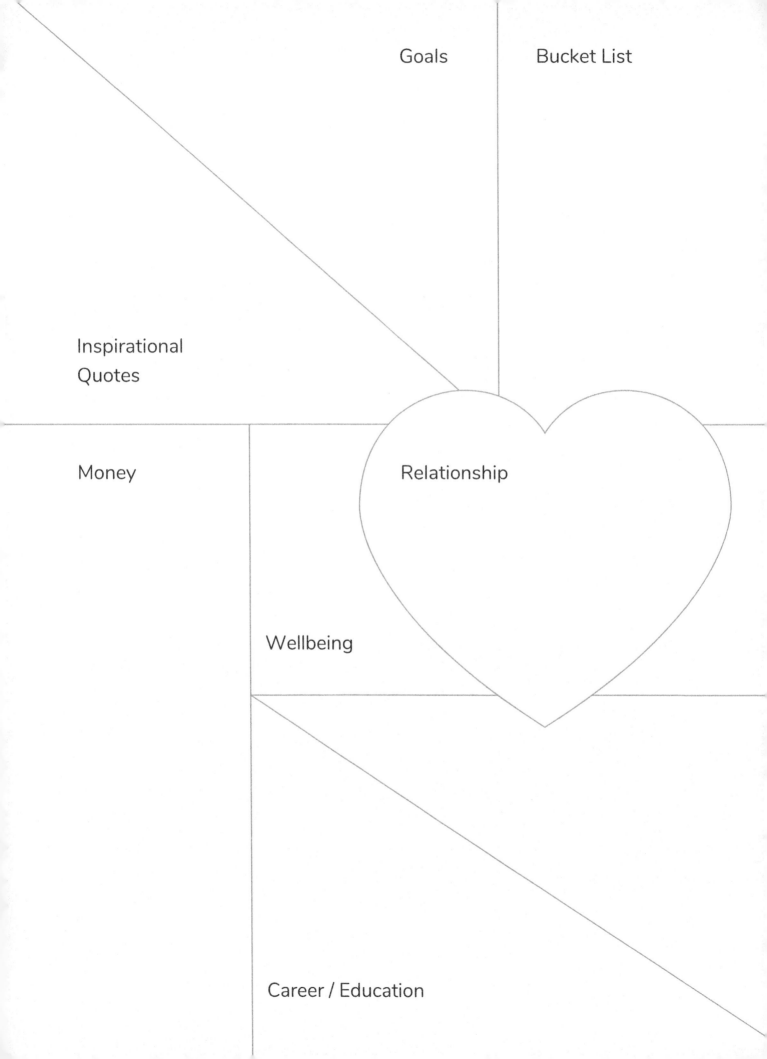

Goals

Bucket List

Inspirational
Quotes

Money

Relationship

Wellbeing

Career / Education

Relationship Communications

Problem I would like to solve

My desired outcome

What do I feel
about this issue?

What do I think my partner feels
about this issue?

What do I feel I need to do to
solve this problem?

What do I feel my partner needs
to do to solve this problem?

What would I like my partner to do today

What I would like to do today

What obstacles are
in our way?

What strategies can we use to
overcome the obstacles?

What I would like to
tell my partner

Happy Memory Clouds

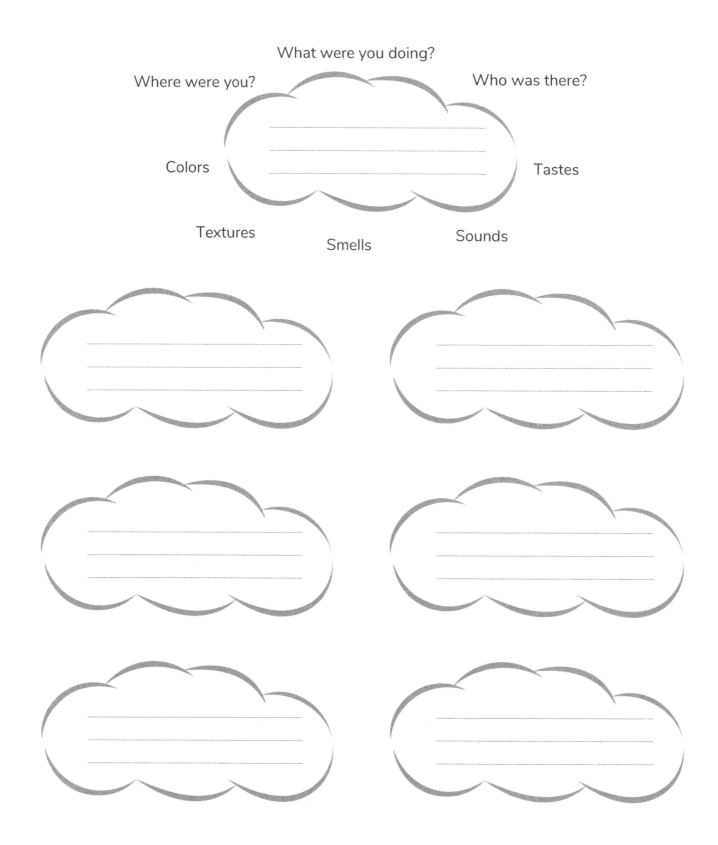

Where were you?   What were you doing?   Who was there?

Colors   Tastes

Textures   Smells   Sounds

Fill out these clouds as you think of happy memories.
Use them when your emotions become overwhelming.

Finger Labyrinth

Use your finger to slowly trace a path to the center of the labyrinth

Breathe calmly and slowly as you focus.
When you reach the center, draw a long deep breath or two.

Then trace your path back to the outside
Repeat until you feel more focused and calm.

Focus Words

Breathe - Peace - Relax - Tranquility - Serenity - Calm - Space - Beauty
Love - Wonder - Kindness - Light - Happiness - Joy - Warmth

Observations

Letting Go
Self Criticism

Critical Thought

"I should…"
"I can't believe…"
"I wish…"
"I'm so stupid"

What triggered this thought?

"I was late to the meeting"
"I forgot to call my mom"
"My friend stood me up"

Physical and Emotional Sensations

How does this thought
make you feel?

Compassionate Thought

What you might say if a
friend expressed this
thought

A year from now

How will you feel about
this event next year?
Will it matter?

Concrete Plan

What action can you
take to prepare for
this in future.

Big picture plan

Imagine a future free
from this thought.
What will you do?

Date _____   Source of Anxiety _____

Time _____   Physical Sensations _____

Place _____

Negative Beliefs

About Yourself	About Situation

What facts do you know are true?

About Yourself	About Situation

Color where you feel
sensations of anxiety

Is there a more balanced way to think about this situation

What has helped before?   ## What is helping now?

Coping Mechanisms

Breathe
Remind yourself that anxiety is just a feeling
Describe your surroundings in detail
Go outdoors
Sip a warm or iced drink slowly
Ground yourself

Self Care Routine

Vision _____

Time	Step

┌─ Routine Notes ─────────────────────────────────

Food _____
_____

Spiritual _____
_____

Exercise _____
_____

Mantra _____

Daily Tracker

1	2	3	4	5	6	7	8	9	10
11	12	13	14	15	16	17	18	19	20
21	22	23	24	25	26	27	28	29	30
31	Start Date :				End Date :				

Date _____   Source of Anxiety _____

Time _____   Physical Sensations _____

Place _____

Negative Beliefs

About Yourself	About Situation

What facts do you know are true?

About Yourself	About Situation

Color where you feel
sensations of anxiety

Is there a more balanced way to think about this situation

What has helped before?

What is helping now?

Coping Mechanisms

Breathe
Remind yourself that anxiety is just a feeling
Describe your surroundings in detail
Go outdoors
Sip a warm or iced drink slowly
Ground yourself

This Week's Goals

What I would like to learn

How I will have fun

Kind things I can do

Places I would like to go

How I will feed my brain

How I will care for my body

Stop stressing about...

Ideas

Conversations

Shopping list

-
-
-
-
-
-
-
-
-
-

Things to do

Explore and learn about...

Goals

Bucket List

Inspirational
Quotes

Money

Relationship

Wellbeing

Career / Education

Relationship Communications

Problem I would like to solve

My desired outcome

What do I feel
about this issue?

What do I think my partner feels
about this issue?

What do I feel I need to do to
solve this problem?

What do I feel my partner needs
to do to solve this problem?

What would I like my partner to do today

What I would like to do today

What obstacles are
in our way?

What strategies can we use to
overcome the obstacles?

What I would like to
tell my partner

Happy Memory Clouds

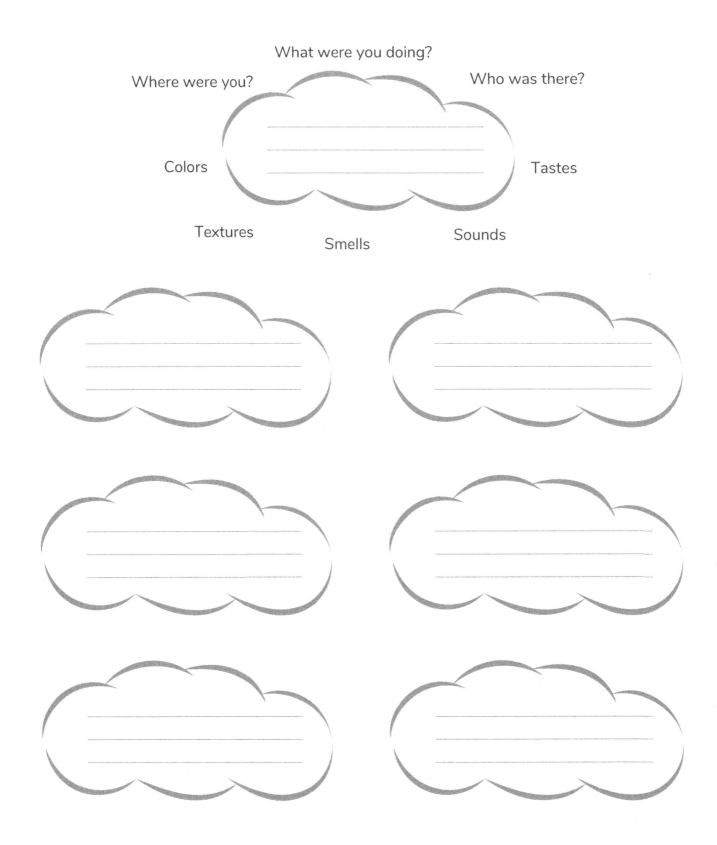

What were you doing?

Where were you?

Who was there?

Colors

Tastes

Textures

Smells

Sounds

Fill out these clouds as you think of happy memories.
Use them when your emotions become overwhelming.

Finger Labyrinth

Use your finger to slowly trace a path to the center of the labyrinth

Breathe calmly and slowly as you focus.
When you reach the center, draw a long deep breath or two.

Then trace your path back to the outside
Repeat until you feel more focused and calm.

Focus Words

Breathe - Peace - Relax - Tranquility - Serenity - Calm - Space - Beauty
Love - Wonder - Kindness - Light - Happiness - Joy - Warmth

Observations

Letting Go
Self Criticism

Critical Thought

"I should…"
"I can't believe…"
"I wish…"
"I'm so stupid"

What triggered this thought?

"I was late to the meeting"
"I forgot to call my mom"
"My friend stood me up"

Physical and Emotional Sensations

How does this thought
make you feel?

Compassionate Thought

What you might say if a
friend expressed this
thought

A year from now

How will you feel about
this event next year?
Will it matter?

Concrete Plan

What action can you
take to prepare for
this in future.

Big picture plan

Imagine a future free
from this thought.
What will you do?

Date _____   Source of Anxiety _____

Time _____   Physical Sensations _____

Place _____

Negative Beliefs

About Yourself	About Situation

What facts do you know are true?

About Yourself	About Situation

Color where you feel
sensations of anxiety

Is there a more balanced way to think about this situation

What has helped before?   What is helping now?

Coping Mechanisms

Breathe
Remind yourself that anxiety is just a feeling
Describe your surroundings in detail
Go outdoors
Sip a warm or iced drink slowly
Ground yourself

Self Care Routine

Vision _____

Time	Step

Routine Notes

Food _____

_____

Spiritual _____

_____

Exercise _____

_____

Mantra _____

Daily Tracker

1	2	3	4	5	6	7	8	9	10
11	12	13	14	15	16	17	18	19	20
21	22	23	24	25	26	27	28	29	30

31	Start Date :	End Date :

Date _____   Source of Anxiety _____

Time _____   Physical Sensations _____

Place _____

Negative Beliefs

About Yourself	About Situation

What facts do you know are true?

About Yourself	About Situation

Color where you feel
sensations of anxiety

Is there a more balanced way to think about this situation

What has helped before?

What is helping now?

Coping Mechanisms

Breathe
Remind yourself that anxiety is just a feeling
Describe your surroundings in detail
Go outdoors
Sip a warm or iced drink slowly
Ground yourself

This Week's Goals

What I would like to learn

How I will have fun

Kind things I can do

Places I would like to go

How I will feed my brain

How I will care for my body

Stop stressing about...

Ideas

Conversations

Shopping list

-
-
-
-
-
-
-
-
-

Things to do

Explore and learn about...

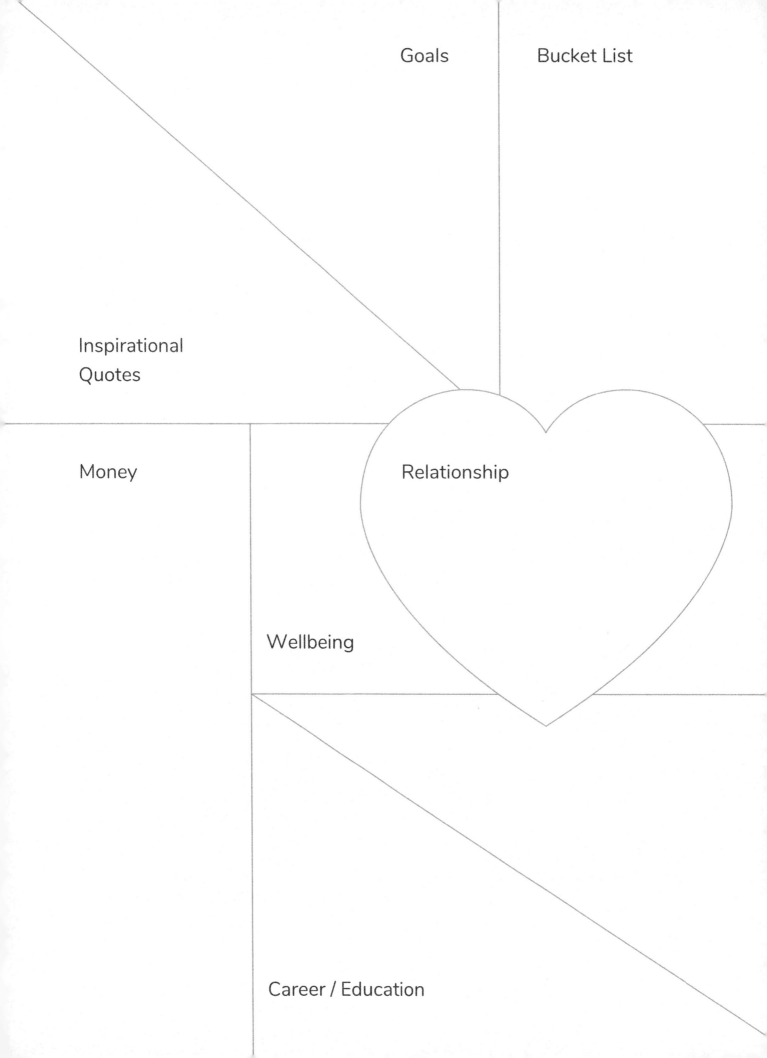

Goals

Bucket List

Inspirational
Quotes

Money

Relationship

Wellbeing

Career / Education

Relationship Communications

Problem I would like to solve

My desired outcome

What do I feel about this issue?

What do I think my partner feels about this issue?

What do I feel I need to do to solve this problem?

What do I feel my partner needs to do to solve this problem?

What would I like my partner to do today

What I would like to do today

What obstacles are in our way?

What strategies can we use to overcome the obstacles?

What I would like to tell my partner

Happy Memory Clouds

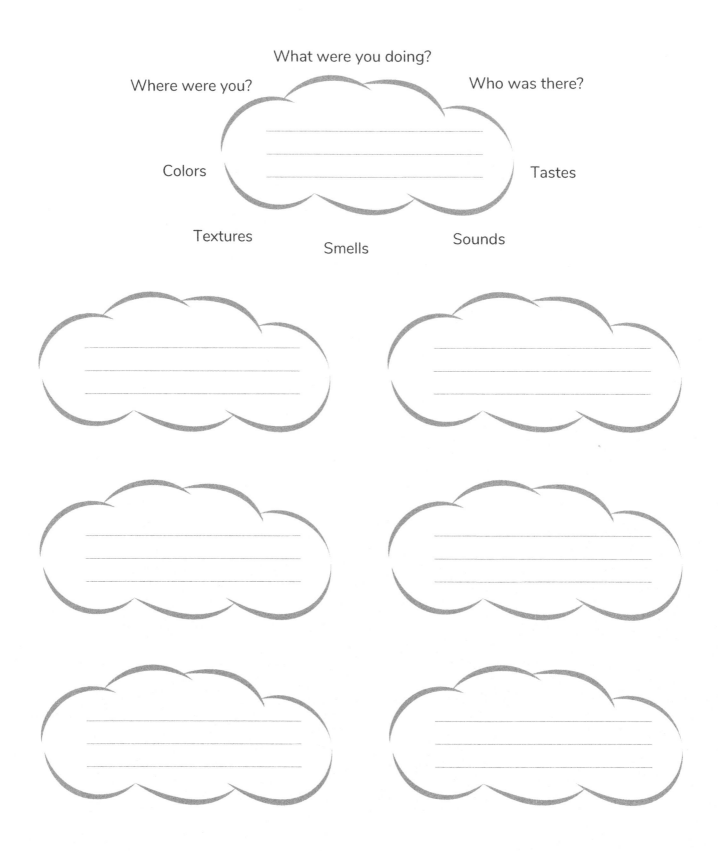

What were you doing?

Where were you?

Who was there?

Colors

Tastes

Textures

Smells

Sounds

Fill out these clouds as you think of happy memories.
Use them when your emotions become overwhelming.

Finger Labyrinth

Use your finger to slowly trace a path to the center of the labyrinth

Breathe calmly and slowly as you focus.
When you reach the center, draw a long deep breath or two.

Then trace your path back to the outside
Repeat until you feel more focused and calm.

Focus Words

Breathe - Peace - Relax - Tranquility - Serenity - Calm - Space - Beauty
Love - Wonder - Kindness - Light - Happiness - Joy - Warmth

Observations

Letting Go
Self Criticism

Critical Thought

"I should..."
"I can't believe..."
"I wish..."
"I'm so stupid"

What triggered this thought?

"I was late to the meeting"
"I forgot to call my mom"
"My friend stood me up"

Physical and Emotional Sensations

How does this thought
make you feel?

Compassionate Thought

What you might say if a
friend expressed this
thought

A year from now

How will you feel about
this event next year?
Will it matter?

Concrete Plan

What action can you
take to prepare for
this in future.

Big picture plan

Imagine a future free
from this thought.
What will you do?

Date _____   Source of Anxiety _____

Time _____   Physical Sensations _____

Place _____

Negative Beliefs

About Yourself	About Situation

What facts do you know are true?

About Yourself	About Situation

Color where you feel
sensations of anxiety

Is there a more balanced way to think about this situation

What has helped before?

What is helping now?

Coping Mechanisms

Breathe
Remind yourself that anxiety is just a feeling
Describe your surroundings in detail
Go outdoors
Sip a warm or iced drink slowly
Ground yourself

Self Care Routine

Vision _____

Time	Step

Routine Notes

Food _____

_____

Spiritual _____

_____

Exercise _____

_____

Mantra _____

Daily Tracker

1	2	3	4	5	6	7	8	9	10
11	12	13	14	15	16	17	18	19	20
21	22	23	24	25	26	27	28	29	30
31	Start Date :				End Date :				

Date _____   Source of Anxiety _____

Time _____   Physical Sensations _____

Place _____

Negative Beliefs

About Yourself	About Situation

What facts do you know are true?

About Yourself	About Situation

Color where you feel
sensations of anxiety

Is there a more balanced way to think about this situation

What has helped before?

What is helping now?

Coping Mechanisms

Breathe
Remind yourself that anxiety is just a feeling
Describe your surroundings in detail
Go outdoors
Sip a warm or iced drink slowly
Ground yourself

This Week's Goals

What I would like to learn

How I will have fun

Kind things I can do

Places I would like to go

How I will feed my brain

How I will care for my body

Stop stressing about...

Ideas

Conversations

Shopping list

- •
- •
- •
- •
- •
- •
- •
- •
- •
- •

Things to do

Explore and learn about...

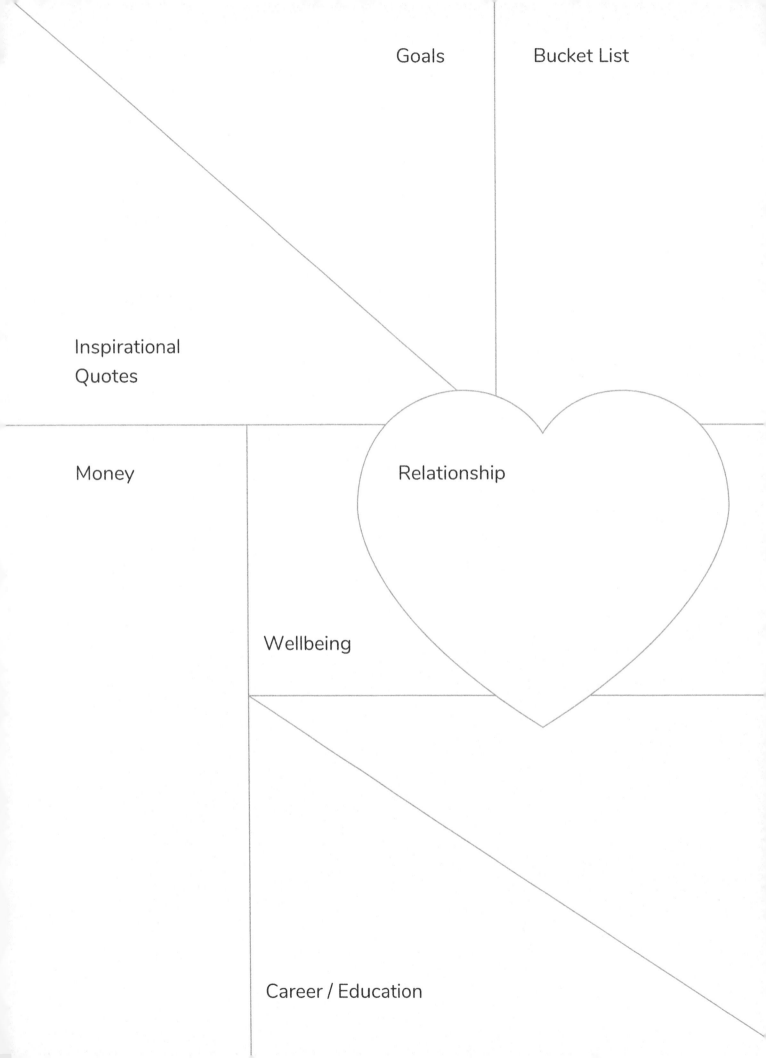

Goals

Bucket List

Inspirational
Quotes

Money

Relationship

Wellbeing

Career / Education

Relationship Communications

Problem I would like to solve

My desired outcome

What do I feel
about this issue?

What do I think my partner feels
about this issue?

What do I feel I need to do to
solve this problem?

What do I feel my partner needs
to do to solve this problem?

What would I like my partner to do today

What I would like to do today

What obstacles are
in our way?

What strategies can we use to
overcome the obstacles?

What I would like to
tell my partner

Happy Memory Clouds

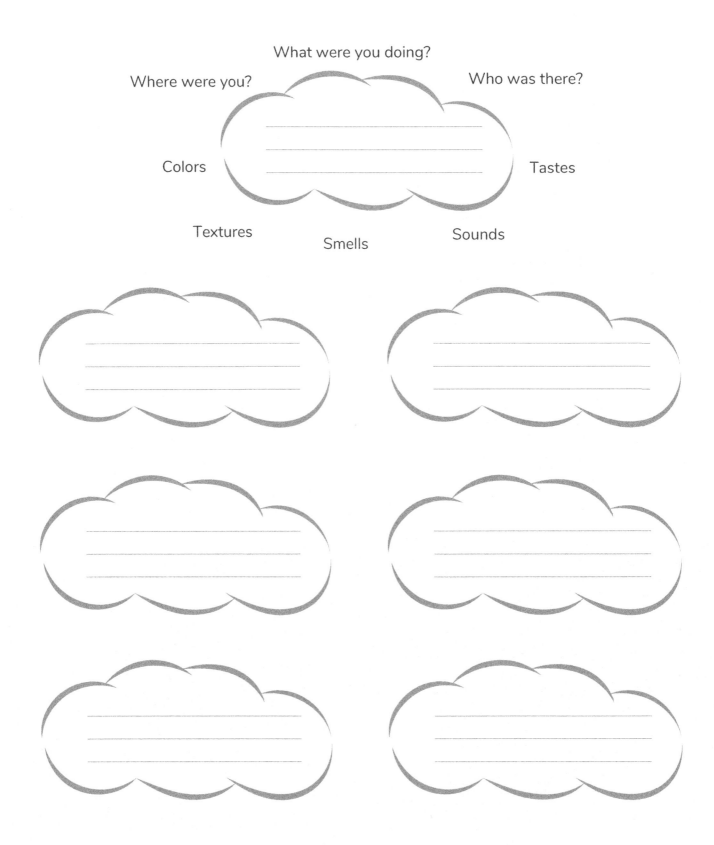

Where were you?
What were you doing?
Who was there?
Colors
Tastes
Textures
Smells
Sounds

Fill out these clouds as you think of happy memories.
Use them when your emotions become overwhelming.

Finger Labyrinth

Use your finger to slowly trace a path to the center of the labyrinth

Breathe calmly and slowly as you focus.
When you reach the center, draw a long deep breath or two.

Then trace your path back to the outside
Repeat until you feel more focused and calm.

Focus Words

Breathe - Peace - Relax - Tranquility - Serenity - Calm - Space - Beauty
Love - Wonder - Kindness - Light - Happiness - Joy - Warmth

Observations

Letting Go
Self Criticism

Critical Thought

"I should..."
"I can't believe..."
"I wish..."
"I'm so stupid"

What triggered this thought?

"I was late to the meeting"
"I forgot to call my mom"
"My friend stood me up"

Physical and Emotional Sensations

How does this thought
make you feel?

Compassionate Thought

What you might say if a
friend expressed this
thought

A year from now

How will you feel about
this event next year?
Will it matter?

Concrete Plan

What action can you
take to prepare for
this in future.

Big picture plan

Imagine a future free
from this thought.
What will you do?

Date _____   Source of Anxiety _____

Time _____   Physical Sensations _____

Place _____

Negative Beliefs

About Yourself	About Situation

What facts do you know are true?

About Yourself	About Situation

Color where you feel
sensations of anxiety

Is there a more balanced way to think about this situation

What has helped before?

What is helping now?

Coping Mechanisms

Breathe
Remind yourself that anxiety is just a feeling
Describe your surroundings in detail
Go outdoors
Sip a warm or iced drink slowly
Ground yourself

Self Care Routine

Vision _____

Time	Step

Routine Notes

Food _____

_____

Spiritual _____

_____

Exercise _____

_____

Mantra _____

Daily Tracker

1	2	3	4	5	6	7	8	9	10
11	12	13	14	15	16	17	18	19	20
21	22	23	24	25	26	27	28	29	30
31	Start Date :				End Date :				

Printed in Great Britain
by Amazon

23720116R00057